HOW TO Draw Type AND INFLUENCE PEOPLE

AN ACTIVITY BOOK

Published in 2017 by
Laurence King Publishing Ltd
361–373 City Road
London EC1V 1LR
United Kingdom
tel +44 20 7841 6900
fax +44 20 7841 6910
email: enquiries@laurenceking.com
www.laurenceking.com

A catalogue record for this book is
available from the British Library

ISBN: 978-1-78067-975-4

Design by Alexandre Coco

The body text of this book
is set in Franklin Gothic

Printed in China

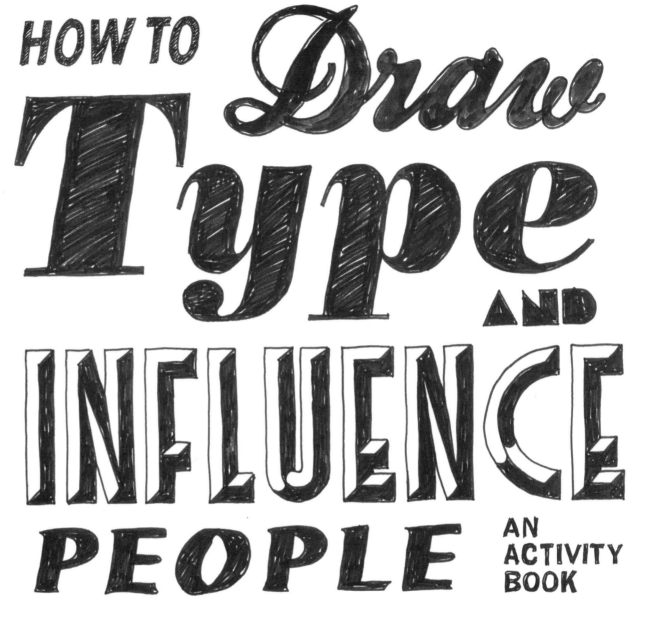

HOW TO Draw Type AND INFLUENCE PEOPLE

AN ACTIVITY BOOK

Sarah Hyndman

Laurence King Publishing

VICTORIAN ADORNMENT

Choose these grand, decorated styles to stand out from the crowd or make a big statement with a flourish.

WILD WILD WEST

Use these typefaces when you want to add a touch of the pioneering Wild West spirit.

I COME FROM OUTER SPACE

Use these typefaces to create a stylized glimpse of the future, or to reflect a nostalgic Space Age from times gone by.

Painted by Hand

Choose a typeface with a sign-painted style for occasions when you want individual flair and a craftsman's touch.

S for Style

Use these typefaces when you wish to exude effortless style and elegance.

MIXED TYPE

Choose a typeface that adds layers of meaning to a word, or deconstruct the letters for an unexpected twist.

REBEL REBEL

Use type to break the rules and to start your own personal revolution.

INTRODUCTION

TYPE IS ALL AROUND US

We are all type consumers and we interact with typefaces frequently as we go about our everyday lives. We may not be consciously aware of it, but the shapes and styles of the fonts themselves communicate a huge amount of information independently of the words they spell out. We instinctively understand what they are communicating to us because we have been learning to recognize these visual codes all our lives.

Every time we see a font we remember the context we saw it in and this gradually builds into a comprehensive library of associations we can refer to. Some of these might be universally shared associations, others will be a result of our own unique and personal experiences.

A font has the power to transform the meaning of a word: to give it a voice and a personality, to make it look knowledgeable, extrovert or stylish. Fonts keep us safe and help us find our way, and sometimes perform a sleight of hand. Fonts interact with all our senses, giving us a glimpse of what a product might taste or smell like and how much it will cost when we buy it – just compare the items of confectionery illustrated here with those illustrated on the page opposite.

FONT OR TYPEFACE?

A typeface is the design of the letter that you see. A font is the delivery mechanism – this could be a metal printing plate or a file on your computer. To compare this to music, a typeface is the equivalent of a song, and a font is the medium by which you listen to it, which could be a vinyl record, a cassette tape or a file on your computer.

However, while professionals consider it important to use the correct terminology, the two terms are becoming increasingly interchangeable. I think we should all enjoy talking about our experience of type without worrying about using the 'correct' words.

A visual glossary explaining all the technical terms used in this book can be found on pages 120–125.

Helvetica Light

WHICH WOULD YOU BUY?

For each of the products shown here,
choose the one you would be most likely
to buy, basing your choice on the typeface.

Colour in the packaging.

Bodoni Poster Italic

Playbill

Bauhaus

Candice

Bodoni Poster Italic

Brody

Playbill

Bauhaus

Brody

Candice

DRAW WHAT YOU SEE

Take a look around you at the products you can see. Draw their logos and the product names on these pages.

A family affair

Choose a typeface with an extended family to give you a broad vocal range to draw on.

This is useful for projects where you would like a range of expression from quiet and subtle to loud and attention-seeking, and to create complex levels of hierarchy within a document.

Largest to smallest: Weights of Helvetica Neue – Bold Extended, Medium Extended, Extended, Thin, Ultra Light Condensed, Ultra Light Condensed Oblique

TYPEFACE FAMILIES

A typeface family gives you an extensive vocal range. With just one typeface you can communicate a wide range of expressions and emotions.

A traditional type family generally includes roman, italic and bold styles. An extended family will include additional weights and widths (e.g. Helvetica, Univers), and a super family might include both sans serif and serif styles (e.g. Scala Pro, Thesis).

TYPE KARAOKE

Read each 'hello' out loud in the style it suggests to you. Try this out on friends and see if they respond in the same way – it's also a fun game to play with kids.

This demonstrates that we know instinctively what different weights, sizes and styles of fonts might sound like, that type visually represents our voice.

1.

2.

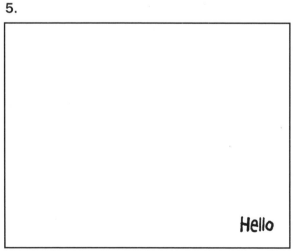

3.

4.

5.

6.

The extended Univers family

TYPE ELOCUTION

Colour in each 'voice' so it looks like it would sound different. Choose the lines to fill in, from light to bold or italic. You could choose to mix and match the letter weights.

The extended Univers family

I'm talking to YOU

Baseline

VISUAL ONOMATOPOEIA

The opposite page has all the letters needed to create the phrase 'I'm talking to you' in a number of different weights and styles of the extended Univers family, from Univers Thin Ultra Condensed through to Univers Extra Black.

1. Cut the page out along the dotted line – be careful not to damage the book's binding.

2. Cut out individual letters and create the phrase 'I'm talking to you' a number of times, so each version looks like it 'sounds' different.

- Mix weights and styles.

- Use spacing to represent the speed each word is spoken at.

- Vary where the letters sit in relation to the baseline to reflect intonation.

- If you want larger or smaller letters, or to modify your letterforms, you can add in hand-drawn elements.

l'agiklmnoottuy l'agiklmnoottuy l'agiklm
noottuy l'agiklmnoottuy l
'agiklmnoottuy l'agiklmn
ototuy l'agiklmnoottu
y l'agiklmnoottuy l'a
giklmnoottuy l'ag
iklmnoottuy l'A
GIKLMNOOTTUY

TOGETHER FOREVER

Combine letterforms to create new icons
or your own unique typographic monogram.

The letterforms of the most frequently used
words can be combined and reduced to a single
ligature, such as æ, the & or @ signs, or letters
that regularly appear together. Doing this with
your own initials enables you to create your own
typographic mark as individual as your signature.

Avant Garde Bold

Mrs Eaves

Mrs Eaves

Avant Garde Bold

LIGATURES

Traditionally ligatures were created for efficiency by combining two frequently used letters to make a single metal printing block. Typesetters selected and placed each individual letter by hand, so this saved them time. The two letters are carefully crafted to create the new glyph (a glyph is a single element in a typeface, such as a letter, number or symbol).

DESIGN A NEW LIGATURE

The @ sign is a ligature that dates back to the 1500s, although we associate it with modern forms of communication. There are various theories about its origin, including merchants combining the letters 'e' and 'a' as the abbreviation for 'each at'.

1. Which words do you use so often that you would like to shorten them into a single character – for instance, 'the', 'yes', 'is'?

2. Write down your words.

3. Look at the letterforms and think of inventive ways in which you could combine them, simplifying them down to a single character.

Typefaces: Umbra, Baskerville Italic, Trebuchet, Edwardian Script, Rosewood, Helvetica

MONOGRAMS

Below is a selection of monograms created by famous Vienna Secession artists around the turn of the 20th century. Each is a unique mark, made from their initials, which identified and authenticated their work.

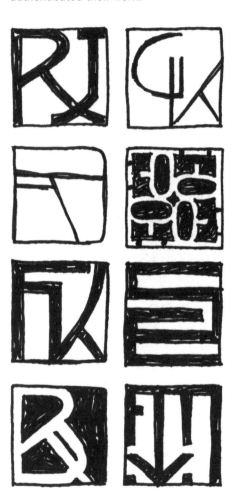

CREATE A PERSONAL MONOGRAM

1. Sketch out variations of your initials in different typefaces in the space below. Try them in upper and lower case, but don't combine them just yet.

2. Put together different combinations to create a selection of monogram ideas in the top row of boxes opposite.

3. Draw your final version in the large box opposite. You could scan this and use it on your stationery or get a rubber stamp made.

ALL THE SENSES

Choose typefaces that trigger all your senses.

You know instinctively what some fonts might smell, taste or feel like from their shapes and the associations you have gathered throughout your life. Much of what you experience actually happens in your brain, which blends information gathered from all your senses.

WHAT WOULD THIS TASTE LIKE?

Candice

THIS IS JUST INK ON PAPER, BUT DO YOU ALSO SEE IT IN 3D?

Macula

WHAT DO YOU THINK THIS WOULD FEEL LIKE TO TOUCH?

Klute

WHAT SCENT DOES THIS SUGGEST TO YOU?

Flemish Script

IF THIS IS A SOUND, WHAT DO YOU HEAR?

Shatter

For more about sound, see page 12

TASTE

The shapes of letterforms can suggest different taste experiences. Round and oozing letters suggest something might taste sweet, while more angular letters could suggest food might be sour or crunchy. We know this from a combination of our instinctive responses to the shapes themselves, and because we have seen particular styles used repeatedly on food and snack packaging.

EAT YOUR WORDS

Invent your own flavours for crisps, fizzy drink and ice cream. These can be new and unusual – think about combining surprising flavours or textures.

1. Think of a name for each of your products.

2. What is the taste experience? For example, is it crunchy, fizzy, popping, cold, melt in the mouth, sweet and/or sour?

3. Draw the name of each product on the appropriate packaging so that the letterforms give a clue to the taste experience.

See page 116 for results from the author's own surveys

TOUCH

It is becoming increasingly important for designers to think about how typefaces might move or what they might feel like to touch with the development of virtual reality and the creation of 3D environments that the viewer can navigate while remaining fully immersed in the experience. As soon as a user experience stops feeling authentic this can make us uncomfortably aware of it, like noticing a badly cast actor in a film.

Considerations are how they will move, how gravity will affect them, how solid they are and what they would feel like to touch.

FEEL THE WORDS

1. Sketch how you think one of the letters would look in 3D from a different perspective.

2. Sketch out how you think it would move, and how it would land if it fell to the ground. Would it be heavy, does it bounce, break or land with a thud?

3. What would it feel like to touch – is it solid or flexible and what temperature might it be? Sketch the texture and materials you think it might be made of – add photos or magazine cuttings where you think these are appropriate.

Candice

Macula

Touch   Touch   Touch

Klute

Flemish Script

Shatter

FONT SNIFFING

What do you think each of these typefaces would smell like?

Smell

Smell

Smell

Smell

Smell

Smell

Smell

Smell

abcdefghijklmnopq
rstuvwxyz

abcdefghijklmnop q
rstuvwxyz

*abcdefghijklmnopqr
stuvwxyz*

**abcdefghijklmnop
qrstuvwxyz**

*abcdefghijklmnopq
rstuvwxyz*

abcdefghijklmnop
qrstuvwxyz

abcdefghijklmno
pqrstuvwxyz

abcdefghijklmnopqrstuv
wxyz

Top to bottom: Candice, Futura Light, Garamond Italic, Bodoni Poster Italic, Flemish Script, Didot, Klute, Onyx

SMELL LABORATORY

1. Think of three strong smells that you have experienced recently – these don't necessarily need to be pleasant smells.

2. Think about how you could represent the smell through your choice of typeface so that somebody might make a good guess at what it is.

3. Write the word 'Smell' on each jar below in letterforms that convey as much as possible about the smell. You can use the alphabets on the opposite page for inspiration.

Font Personalities

It is important to think of personality and tone of voice when choosing a font, not just its legibility.

Imagine that the page opposite represents a room full of people. What assumptions would you make about them from the typefaces, similar to the non-verbal clues you might pick up from their accent and the clothes they are wearing?

F Caslon o Bauhaus n Caslon Italic t Bauhaus
P Bodoni Poster e Caslon Italic f Bauhaus S Caslon O Caslon Italic n Bauhaus a Bodoni Poster l Caslon i Bauhaus t Bodoni Poster i Caslon e Bauhaus s Bauhaus

Write three words to describe the personality of each of these typefaces on the dotted lines.

"Hello"

"Hello"

"Hello"

"Hello"

"Hello"

"Hello"

"Hello"

Clockwise from top right: Bodoni Poster, Cinema Italic, Lubalin Graph, Georgia, Cocon, Apple Chancery, Bauhaus

33

FONT PERSONALITIES

These are a few of the main attributes generally associated with each type personality – can you think of more? See page 117 for answers and more information.

Knowledgeable and skilful
Serifs
Traditional, older-style typefaces
Double-storeyed 'a' and 'g'

Informative and easy
Sans serifs
Larger x-height and open letters

Friendly
Rounded shapes or terminals
Hand-drawn feel, casual not formal
Single-storey 'a' and 'g'

Extrovert
Bold
Stylized

PERSONALITY PROFILING

1. Choose a colour for each type personality and add this to the frame around each title.

2. Look at each of the typefaces indicated by the dotted lines and decide which type personality category you think they fall into. Neatly colour them in the appropriate colour. If you think a typeface fits more than one category then it can be multicoloured to represent this.

Caslon

Bauhaus

Helvetica

Futura

Knowledgeable & skilful

Colour this in

Cocon

Braggadocio

Georgia

Franklin Gothic

VAG Rounded

Cinema Italic

Comic Sans

Baskerville

| Informative & easy | Friendly | Extrovert |

Monotype Corsiva

Bodoni Poster

Garamond

NON-VERBAL COMMUNICATION

Your choice of typeface conveys non-verbal information about what you have written before people have even read your words, in the same way that your clothes communicate a great deal of information about you before you have even started to speak.

1. Think about each of these events and the document or invitation you might design to accompany each one.

2. Select two typefaces from the collection below that you think will be best suited to each scenario.

3. Draw these neatly underneath each of the hangers.

JOB INTERVIEW

1.   2.

Left to right: Baskerville, Brody, Helvetica, Didot, Futura, Comic Sans

36

KIDS' SPORTS DAY

COCKTAIL PARTY

1.

2.

1.

2.

Left to right: Bauhaus, Bodoni Poster Italic, Georgia, Apple Chancery, Stilla, Cooper Black

Fonts of Knowledge

Use a typeface with serifs to convey skill, wisdom and timeless knowledge.

Printed books have been valuable sources of knowledge and learning since the invention of the printing press. They have featured serif typefaces for almost 500 years and as a result these styles have become associated with gravitas, wisdom and knowledge.

Baskerville

Knowledge

CATEGORY: Humanist serifs. The earliest printed serifs, which have a calligraphic feel.

Wisdom

CATEGORY: Old Style serifs. These are a little more refined and less calligraphic.

Intelligence

CATEGORY: Transitional serifs. Often considered the easiest to read of the serifs.

Expertise

CATEGORY: Modern serifs.
Refined, crisp details and hairline serifs.

Top to bottom: Centaur, Caslon, Baskerville, Didot

SERIFS

Serif typefaces have small strokes on the ends of the letters. From their introduction in Europe in the 1400s, they were the most popular style for print for almost 500 years, until sans serif typefaces became popular in the mid-1900s.

Typefaces such as Baskerville and Caslon are associated with learning and knowledge, and are used when a serious tone needs to be conveyed.

CUT OUT AND TRANSFORM

The opposite page has deconstructed versions of the letterforms 'a', 'b' and 'c' in a font from each of the four serif categories outlined on the previous page.

You will need glue and scissors or a craft knife.

1. Cut the page out along the dotted line – be careful not to damage the book's binding.

2. Cut out the shapes along the dotted lines and stick them over the letters below and overleaf to transform them into serifs. You could keep all the shapes from one category together, or mix and match them.

 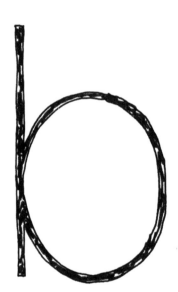 

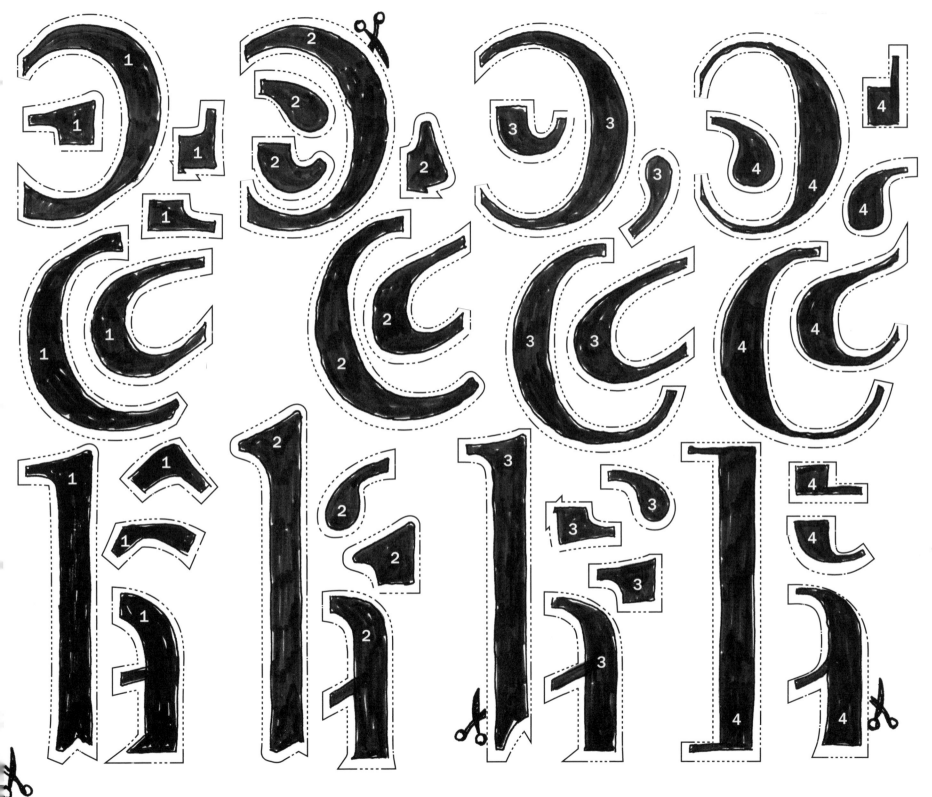

1: Humanist **2:** Old Style **3:** Transitional **4:** Modern

a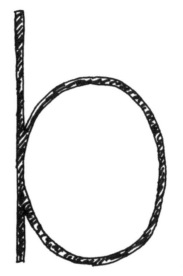

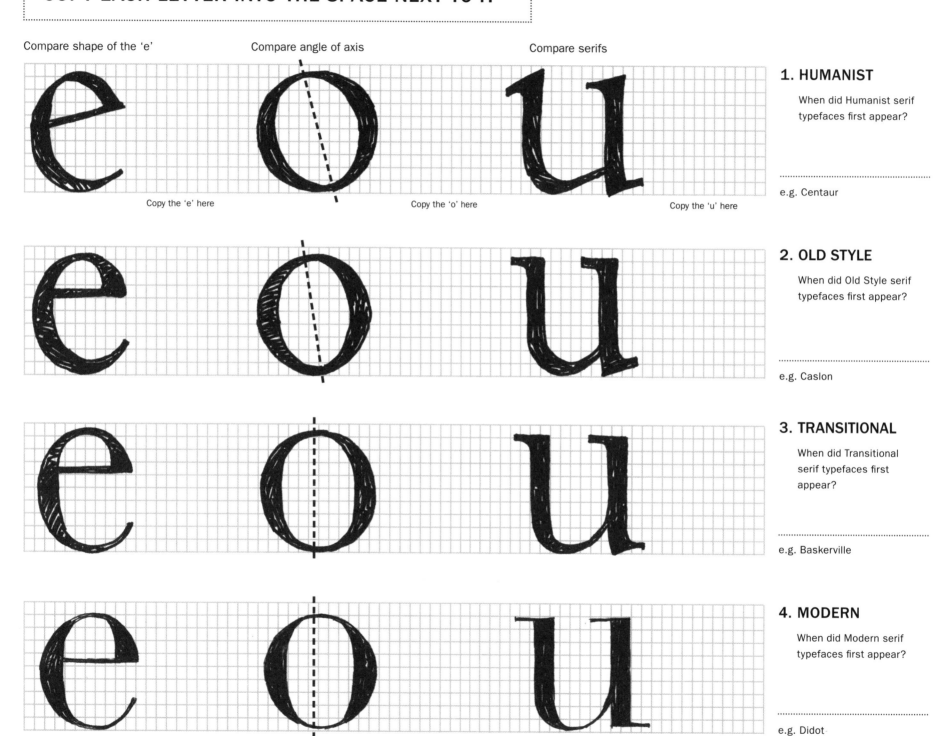

Compare shape of the 'e'

Compare angle of axis

Compare serifs

Copy the 'e' here

Copy the 'o' here

Copy the 'u' here

1. HUMANIST

When did Humanist serif typefaces first appear?

....

e.g. Centaur

2. OLD STYLE

When did Old Style serif typefaces first appear?

....

e.g. Caslon

3. TRANSITIONAL

When did Transitional serif typefaces first appear?

....

e.g. Baskerville

4. MODERN

When did Modern serif typefaces first appear?

....

e.g. Didot

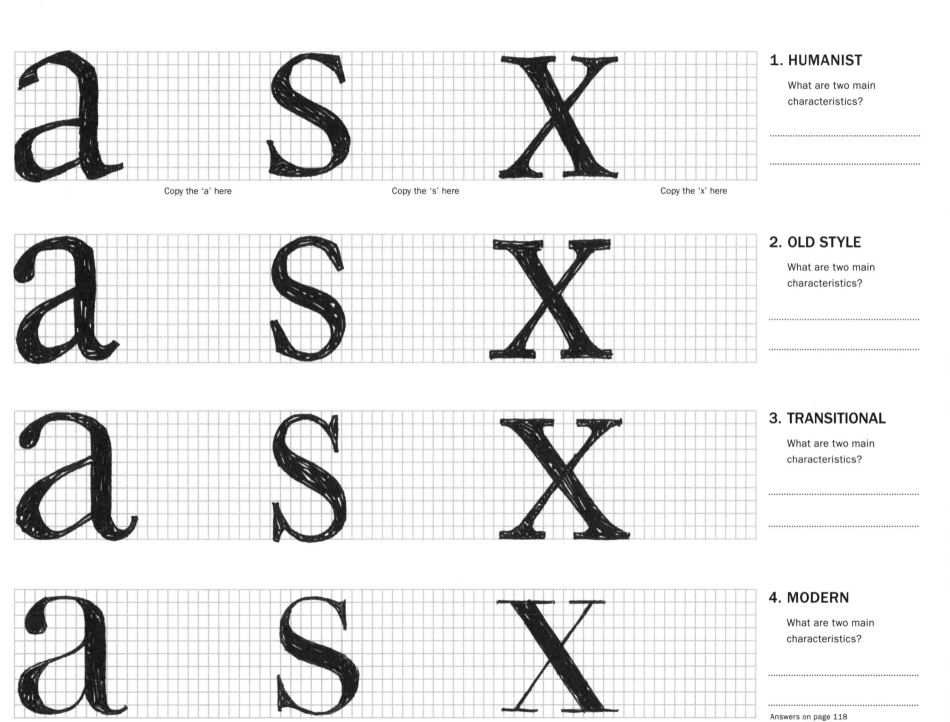

Copy the 'a' here   Copy the 's' here   Copy the 'x' here

1. HUMANIST

What are two main characteristics?

....

....

2. OLD STYLE

What are two main characteristics?

....

....

3. TRANSITIONAL

What are two main characteristics?

....

....

4. MODERN

What are two main characteristics?

....

....

Answers on page 118

Less is More

Use sans serif type styles to communicate quickly and clearly.

No fuss, no frills, no unnecessary embellishments or details – typefaces for when form is to follow function.

Minimal
neutral

&
Functional

Top to bottom: Univers Light, Helvetica, Neue Haas Grotesk Black, Neue Haas Grotesk Light

SANS SERIFS

Sans serif typefaces have letters without strokes or 'serifs' ('sans' means 'without' in French). These pared-down styles first appeared in the 1800s but were considered too different and 'ugly' at first. They became popular in the mid-1900s when they were embraced for their functionality and for being free from the historical 'baggage' of older styles.

Typefaces like Helvetica and Univers were designed to be neutral, and are still used widely today for situations where information needs to be conveyed clearly, such as road signs and instructions.

MAKE SANS SERIF SOUP

Take a black pen and block out the serifs on the lettering of the soup label on the opposite page to turn them into sans serifs.

Once you have done this, compare the two versions:

1. Which soup do you think would be easiest to cook?

2. Which soup do you think will be tastiest?

3. Which soup are you most likely to buy?

Answers on page 119, based on the author's surveys

Caslon Semibold

B

NEO-GROTESQUE

For neutrality, when information is more important than style.

GEOMETRIC

For clean and geometric shapes that convey precision and considered style.

See page 100 to design your own Geometric sans serif typeface

HUMANIST

For a human touch and a slightly hand-drawn style.

See page 52 to draw a Humanist sans serif typeface

GROTESQUE

For information that needs to stand out, with a nod to history.

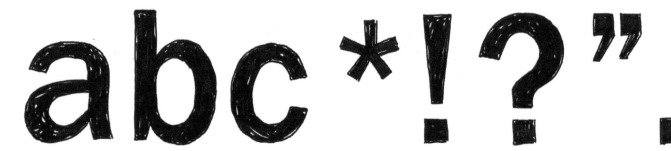

Top to bottom: Helvetica Black, Futura Bold, Gill Sans Bold, Franklin Gothic Medium

Neo-grotesque sans serifs (from 1950s)

Developed from the Grotesque sans serifs of the previous century (see below), but with large families of weights and styles that are designed to work together harmoniously.

e.g. Helvetica, Univers, Folio

FILL IN THE DETAILS:

abcd

Where do you expect to see this style used?

....

....

....

Geometric sans serifs (from 1920s)

In contrast to Humanist sans serifs (see below), these are based on geometric shapes and became popular for their clean and, at the time, modern design. They have a slightly mechanical feel and many of the letters and numbers can look similar at small sizes.

e.g. Futura, Avant Garde, Kabel

abcd

Where do you expect to see this style used?

....

....

....

Humanist sans serifs (from 1916)

Sans serifs with a calligraphic touch. These are often found to be the most legible of the sans serif typefaces owing to their stroke contrast and the clear difference between letters. The earliest examples were created by a calligrapher who was inspired by classic letterforms based on Roman inscriptions.

e.g. Gill Sans, Optima, Frutiger

abcd

Where do you expect to see this style used?

....

....

....

Grotesque sans serifs (from early 1800s)

These were the first sans serifs to appear and were often bold and designed for headlines and advertisements. In their original forms the different widths often look as though they have been designed as different styles, unlike the harmonious extended families of Neo-grotesque sans serifs.

e.g. Franklin Gothic, Akzidenz Grotesk, Monotype Grotesque

abcd

Where do you expect to see this style used?

....

....

....

51

DRAW A HUMANIST SANS SERIF ALPHABET

These letterforms have a hand-drawn feel, which you can see in the varying contrast and shapes of letters such as the 'a' and the 'r', which look a little like they might have been drawn with a calligraphy pen:

Slanted axis

Thick/thin contrast

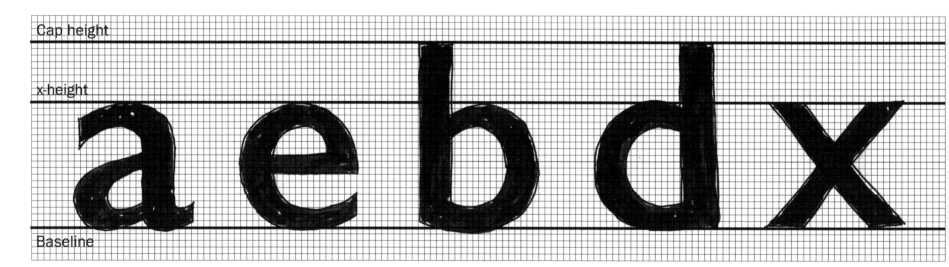

abcdefghij
klmnopqrs
tuvwxyz

Gill Sans

Cap height

x-height

a e b d x

Baseline

EQUIPMENT: RULER, PENCIL

1. Decide how many squares wide each of your letters will be so that they all fit into the same grid.

2. The letters with curves (for example a and e) will need to sit a little over these lines so that they line up with the other letters optically.

3. Design similar shaped letters together so you can copy the shapes from one to the next, for example a and e, b and d.

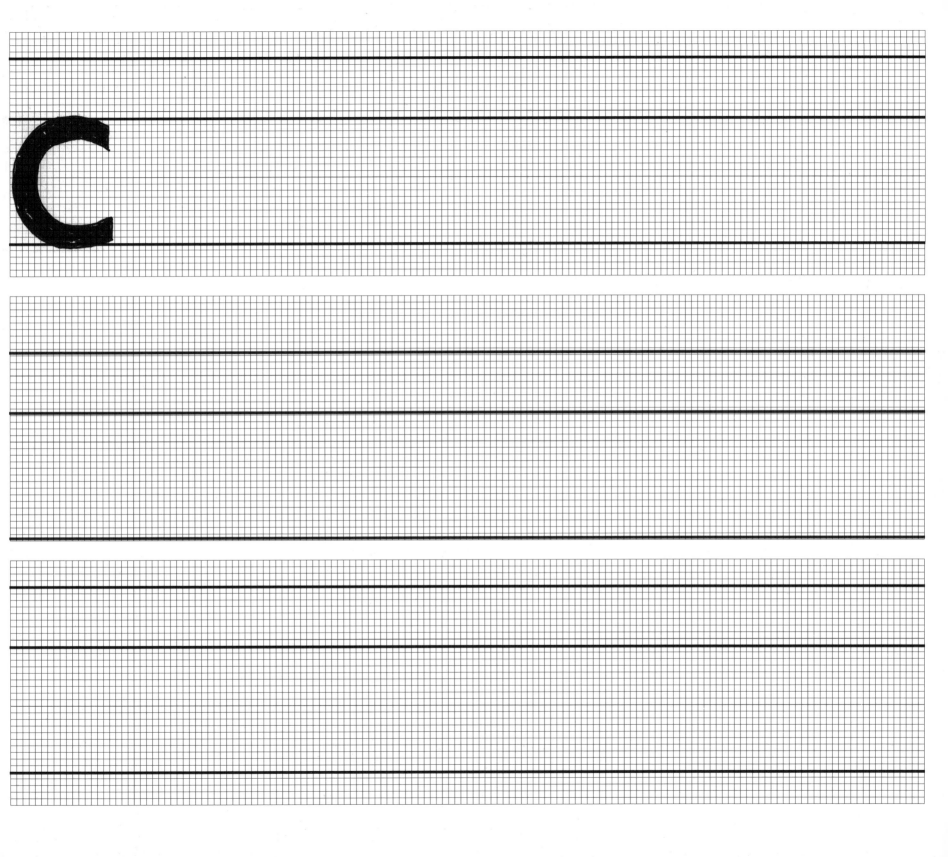

VICTORIAN ADORNMENT

Choose these grand, decorated styles
when you want to stand out from the crowd
or make a big statement with a flourish.

Taking on the role of both word and
image, these letters should appear
as large as possible.

Thorne Shaded

TYPOGRAPHIC EXTRAVAGANCE

In the 1820s, printer Louis John Pouchée created a series of extravagantly decorative typefaces. These were carved from wood and adorned with images of the Victorian era ranging from farmyard scenes to Masonic symbols. They give us a glimpse into the lives and interests of the time.

Pouchée letters, reproduced by permission of St Bride Library & Archives

PACKING A PUNCH

The typeface style that was in vogue in the early 1800s was the Modern style (examples are Didot and Bodoni). This was also an era when the advertising industry was flourishing and most outdoor advertising took the form of large posters and billboards.

The delicate letterforms were a little too lightweight and needed to become bolder if they were to stand out from a distance and in such a visually cluttered environment.

> Trace the evolution of these letters by colouring in the ampersands below. Colour in the shadow of the largest one as well.

LIGHTWEIGHT
Classification: Modern
Examples: Didot, Bodoni

MIDDLEWEIGHT
Classification: Fat Face
Examples: Bodoni Poster

HEAVYWEIGHT
Classification: 3D Fat Face
Examples: Thorne Shaded

DESIGN A MODERN DECORATIVE DISPLAY LETTER

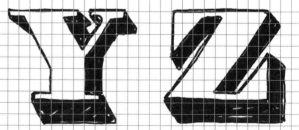

Thorne Shaded

1. Enlarge your chosen letter on the page opposite, using the grid to guide you.

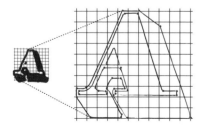

2. Give your letter a modern twist by adding up-to-date images and motifs, or by using collage and mixing together different colours and textures.

3. Repeat this over the next two pages, introducing different motifs or images into the letters.

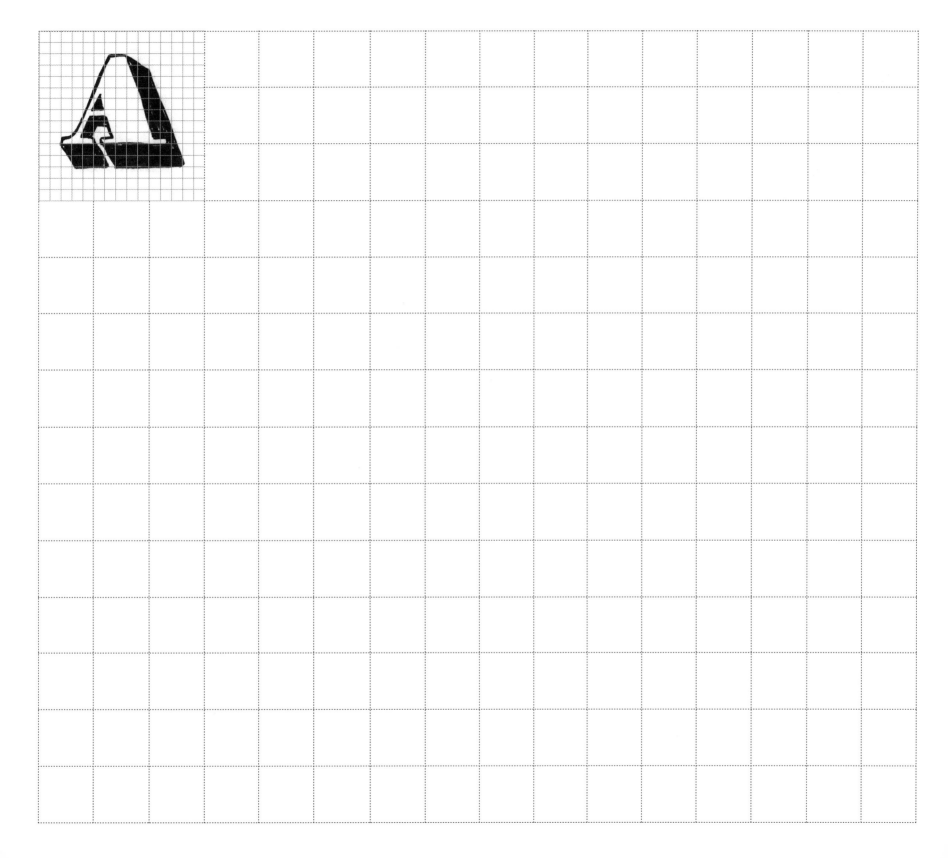

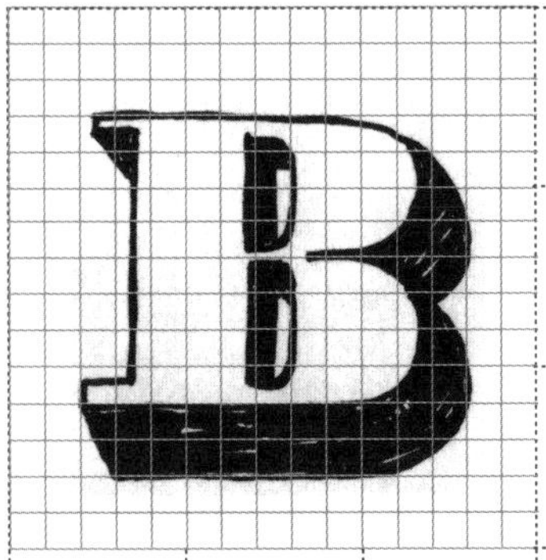

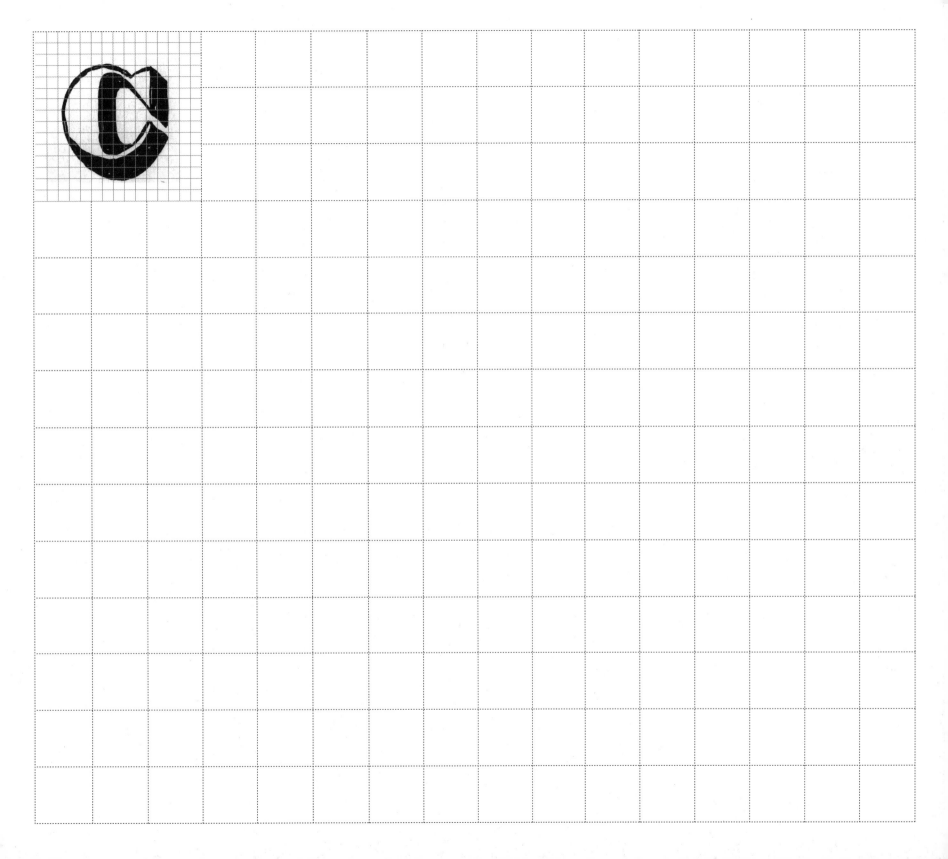

Painted by Hand

Choose a typeface with a sign-painted style for occasions when you want individual flair and a craftsman's touch.

These alphabets originated as one-off signs and advertisements. You can take inspiration from them and use the type to create individual lettering compositions.

Casual Script

Brody

CASUAL

Speedy Casual

SHOW CARD

FLARED

Icone

SERIFS

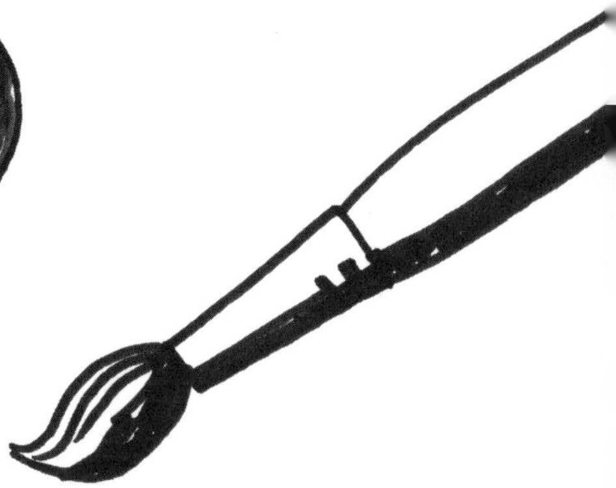

WITH EXTRAS

Algerian

GET ORNATE

Railroad

Get Decadent

Appleton

TYPE VS LETTERING

Sign painting is a skilled craft that became popular in the 18th century as the advertising industry flourished and literacy rates increased.

Often, a sign is a one-off piece with letters designed to fit the space. This is called lettering, and is different from type (fonts), which is a set of letters that can be repeated over and over and always look identical. There are sign painting-style fonts, which are a digitized version of the sign painter's letters.

CASUAL SCRIPT

This is Brody, a casual script inspired by the sign painter's brushwork.

1. With paintbrushes and ink or paint, try out a few different brush sizes and paint textures on a separate piece of paper.

2. Create your own casual script letters in the blank spaces by following the shapes of Brody, but incorporating the natural shapes your own painting style creates.

3. Repeat the same letter a few times to perfect it.

lmnopqrstuvwxyz

FLARED SERIFS

For more formal lettering the sign painter twists the brush to achieve a sharp corner. This has developed as a style in which the twisted shape is exaggerated to form a flared shape (see below).

1. Have a few goes at this on a spare piece of paper using different paintbrush sizes to see which suits you best. Now create your own flared serif letters to the right, repeating just one letter if you wish, until you perfect it.

2. You may want to incorporate your own personalized flourishes that give your alphabet its own unique 'signature'.

Don't worry if your letters are not as neat as the professionals at first, it takes a great deal of practice to perfect the skill.

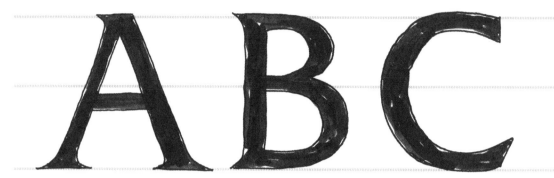

DEFGHIJ

EMBRACING THE MEDIUM

When painting a tall letter, for example on a large sign on a freight car that will be viewed from a distance, the sign painter will need to recharge the paintbrush with paint to complete the vertical stroke.

(a) Try this for yourself. Paint the first 'I', starting at the top, and see if you can paint its entire height without running out of paint.

Once you have recharged your brush and completed the letter, can you see the join? A way to disguise this is to turn the join into a stylistic detail.

(b) Try again with the next 'I', but this time twist your brush halfway down to create an extra detail, then reload it with paint before completing the bottom of the letter.

Continue with (c) and (d), which show how a sign painter's lettering became more ornate.

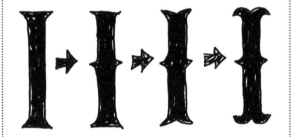

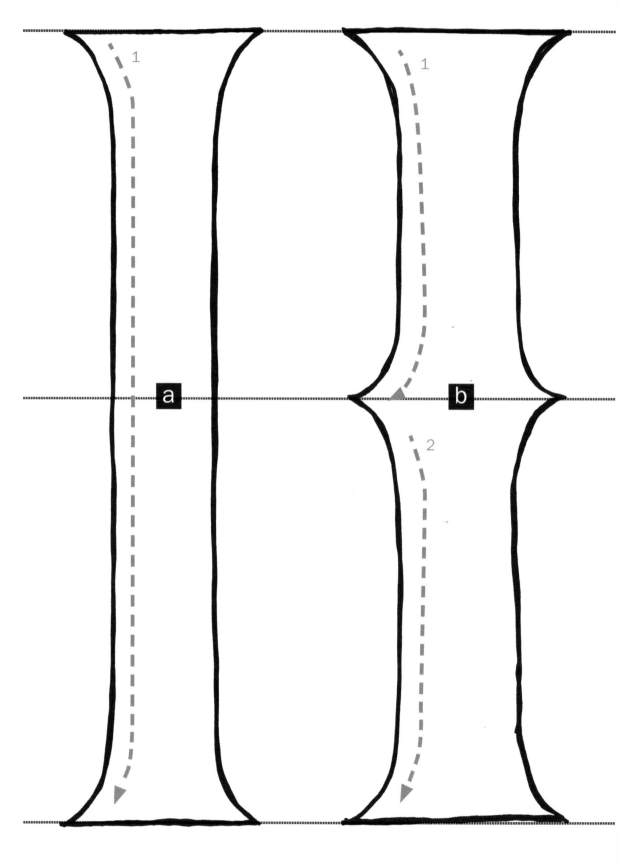

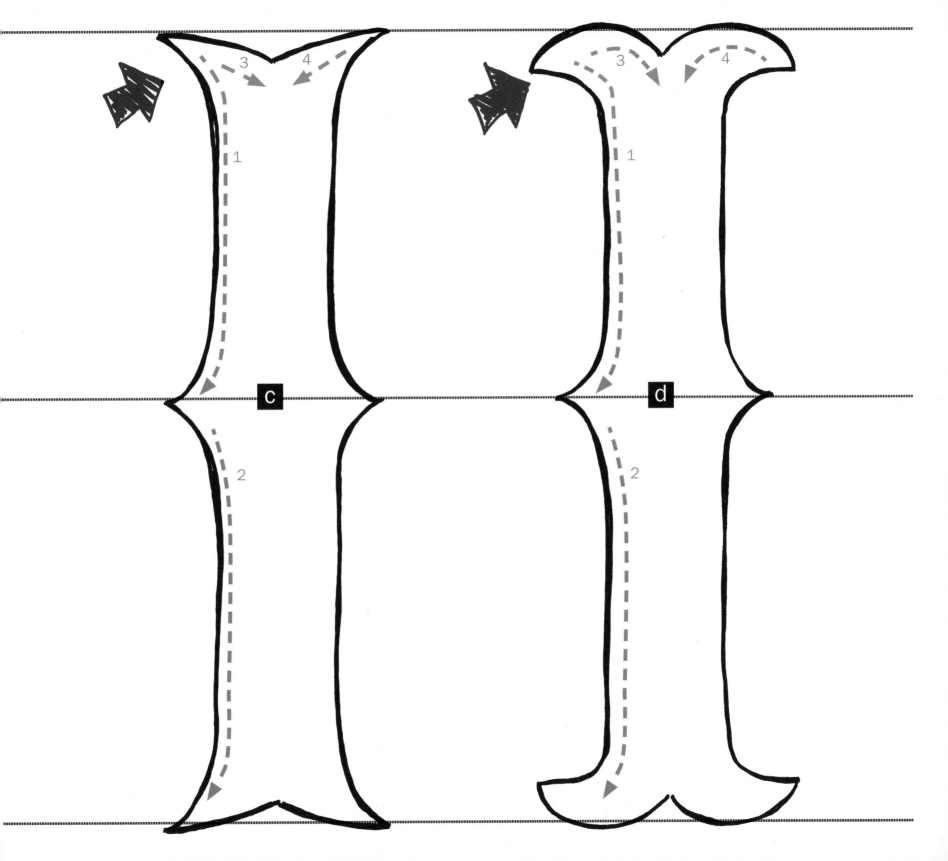

c

d

WILD WILD WEST

Use these typefaces when you want to add
a touch of the pioneering Wild West spirit.

Try combining them with more modern
or minimalist styles to introduce a
contemporary twist.

Branding Iron

WANTED

VICTORIAN
COWBOYS OF THE
WILD WEST
AND
MEXICO

WANTED

Left and right: Stretched Wainwright. **Top to bottom:** Branding Iron, Wainwright/HWT Catchwords, Italienne, Thunderbird, Mesquite

WHO SHOT THE SERIF?

Slab serif typefaces have big, blocky serifs. They were created in Victorian England and exported around the world. They have been used so frequently for 'wanted' posters in Hollywood movies that they have come to be associated with cowboys (e.g. Branding Iron).

Reverse contrast or Italienne slab serifs have horizontal strokes that are thicker than the vertical strokes (e.g. Wainwright).

Catchwords are whole words that were traditionally created as a single printing block. These were often offered alongside standard alphabets in wood type catalogues (e.g. HWT Catchwords).

Tuscan letters are a type of slab serif which have rounded or pointed serifs (e.g. Italienne).

Tuscan type can be very ornate and include extra details halfway down the stem (e.g. Thunderbird).

The plainer Reverse contrast slab serifs are generally associated with the Wild West, while the more ornate Tuscan styles are associated with Mexico (e.g. Mesquite).

Find out more on page 68

ORNATE SLAB SERIFS

These are examples of different styles of slab serifs often associated with Wild West type (although many originated in Victorian England). They range from the simple to the extremely ornate.

Hairline serifs

The vertical strokes are bolder than the horizontal strokes and serifs.

Reverse contrast

The horizontal strokes and serifs are thicker than the vertical strokes.

Design a series of your own ornate slab serifs on the vertical columns below. Which shapes could you incorporate to bring these up to date and reflect more contemporary styles?

A B C D E

F G H I J K

L M N O P

Q R S T U

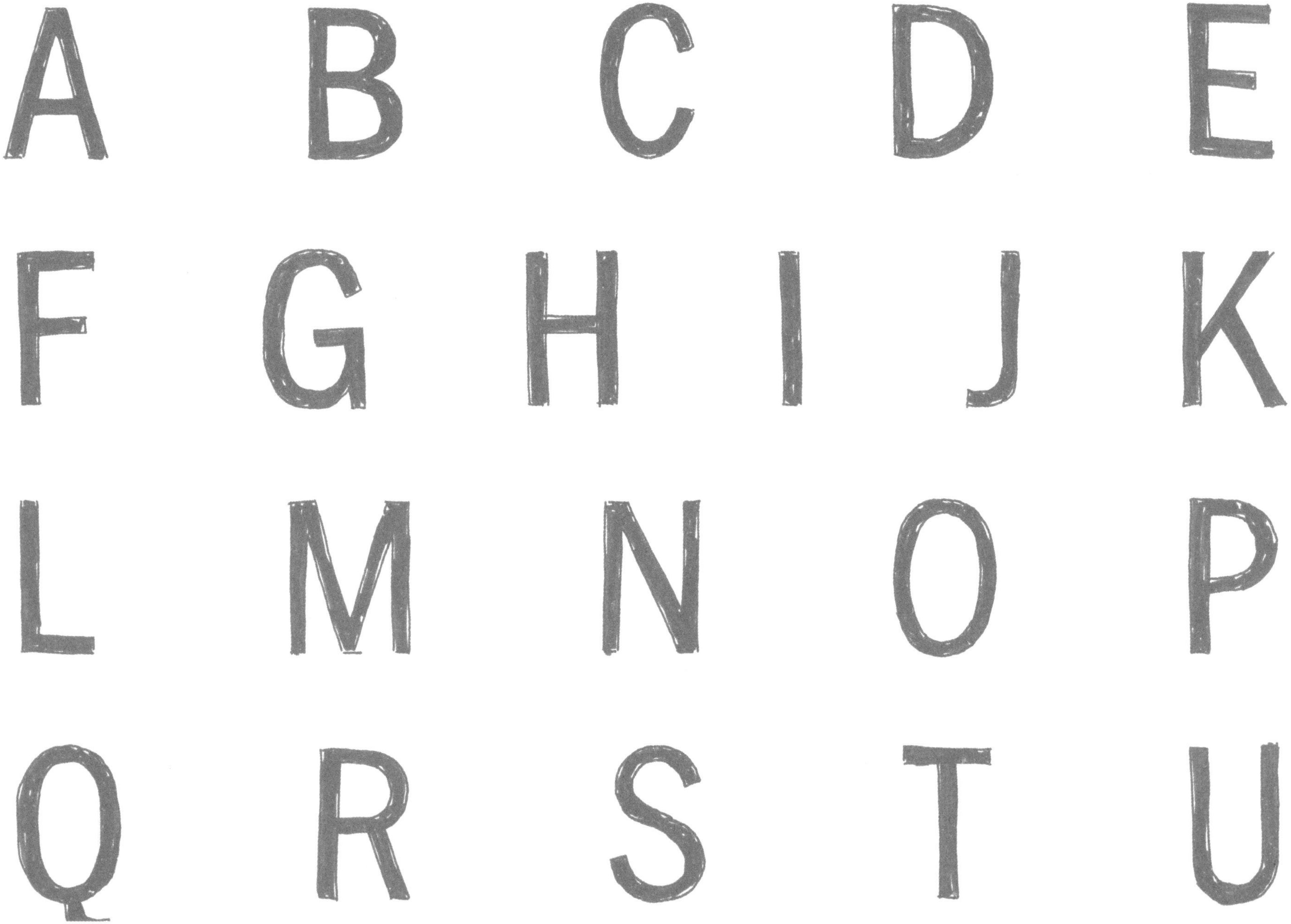

Franklin Gothic Book Condensed

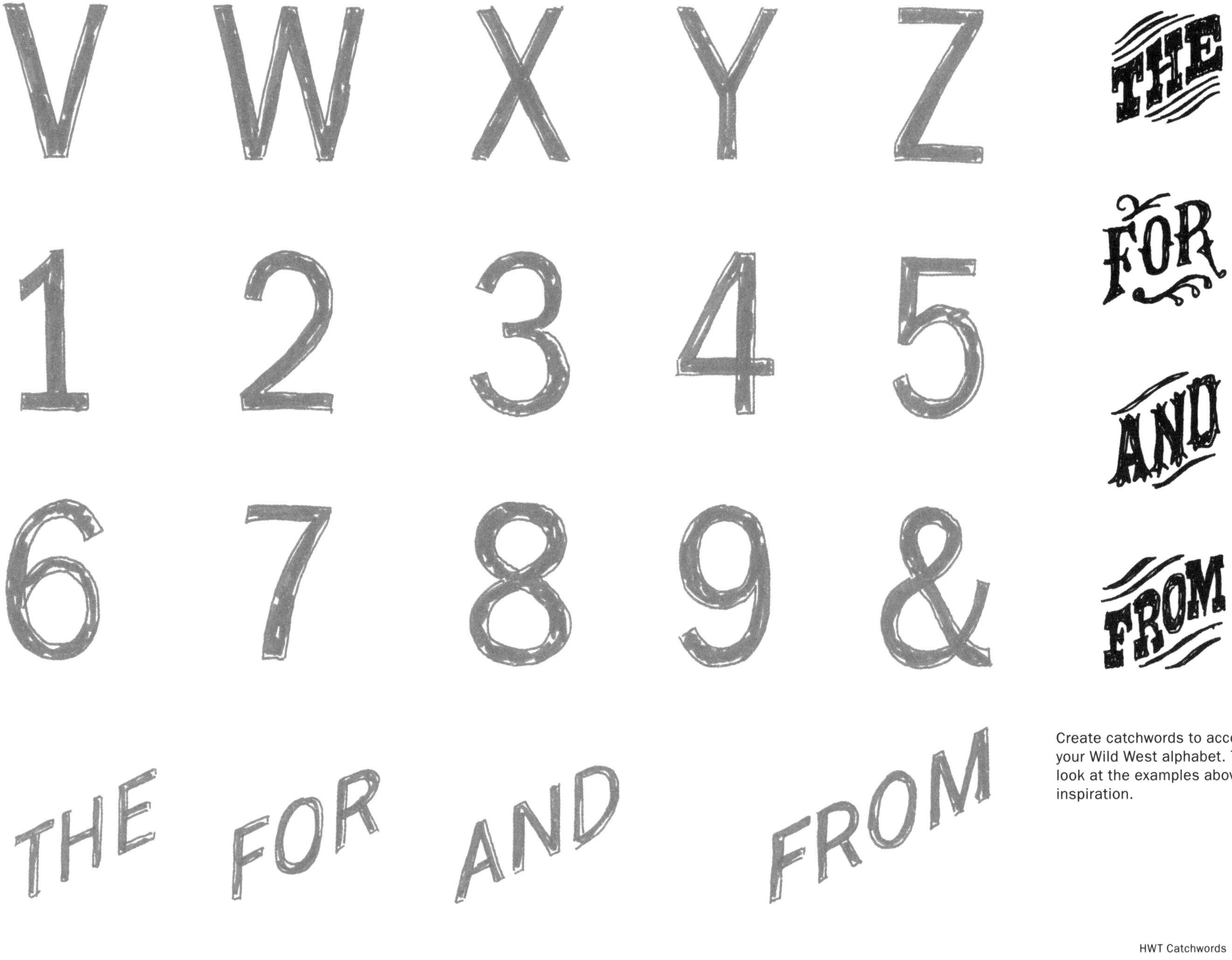

V W X Y Z **THE**

1 2 3 4 5 **FOR**

6 7 8 9 & **AND**

FROM

THE   FOR   AND   FROM

Create catchwords to accompany your Wild West alphabet. Take a look at the examples above for inspiration.

SET UP A WILD WEST APOTHECARY

Invent your own magic potions and design their labels in Wild West styles. Make the names, and what they do, as weird and wonderful as you can imagine.

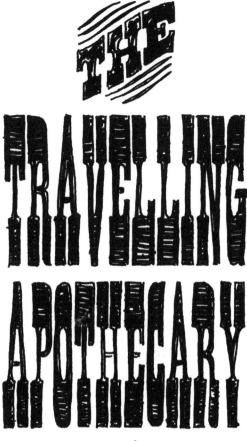

THE TRAVELLING APOTHECARY FOR WONDER CURES AND MAGIC POTIONS

Top to bottom: HWT Catchwords, Wainwright,
HWT Catchwords, Blackoak, HWT Catchwords, Thunderbird

S for Style

Use these typefaces when you wish to exude effortless style and elegance.

Remember to add your own, individual twist though, and don't just be a slavish follower of fashion.

Sophisticated*
CLASSIC*
Elegant*
Stylish*

* Fine details and hairline serifs (Didot).

* These timeless shapes are reminiscent of copperplate engravings from centuries past (Symbol).

* Effortlessly minimal letters inspired by ancient Roman inscriptions but simplified so that they are just a slight hint in the silhouette (Optima).

* The refined contrast of a Didot-style typeface but without the serifs (Chong Light).

FINISHING TOUCHES

It's the fine details and finishing touches that make a difference. Use these shapes as the basis for your own stylish typeface. How minimal will your letterforms be? Will you add razor-sharp serifs, or combine them with completely different shapes to create an innovative new typeface?

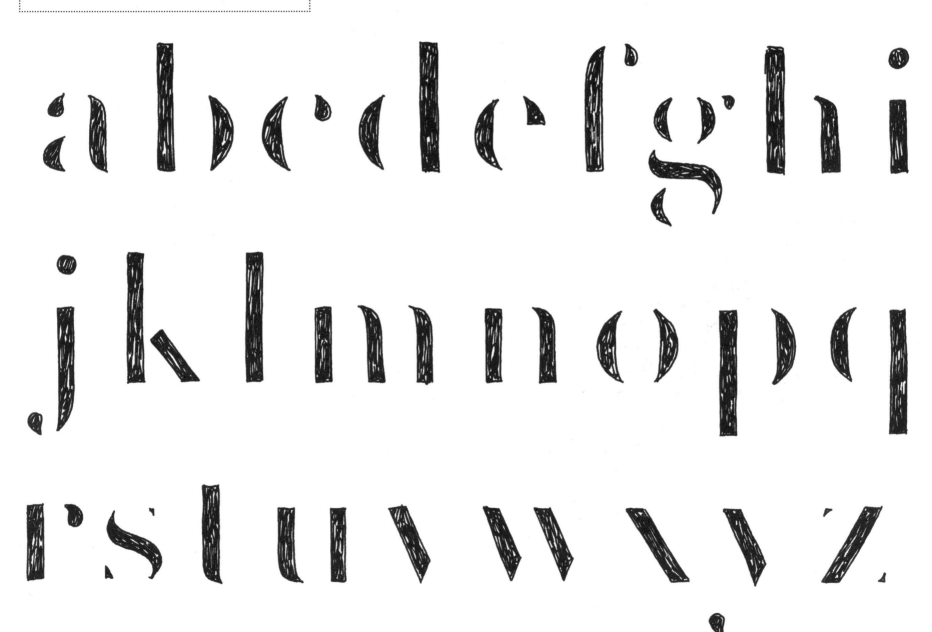

Effortlessly
Understated

CREATE YOUR OWN STYLE MAGAZINE

Create the masthead for the first issue of your own style magazine, which epitomizes elegance and sophistication. Shown here is the cover with just an image waiting for the words to be added.

1. What is the name of your magazine?

2. Where will your masthead appear? It does not have to appear at the top, or even be horizontal – it could interact with the image in some way.

3. Use the typeface you created in the previous exercise. How will the letterforms combine to create the title of your magazine?

4. Try out some ideas as preliminary sketches on the small boxes to the right.

5. When you are ready, measure out the letters in pencil on the large magazine cover opposite before drawing over them in pen.

R E V O L U T I O N

Futura Condensed Extra Bold

East Bloc Open

Use type to break the rules and to start your own personal revolution.

Be inspired by Dada's call for chaos and irrationality, the Futurists' celebration of speed and machines, the Russian Constructivists, who engaged the viewer as an active participant, or Punk, which ripped up the rule book to create a new D.I.Y. style.

ASK
QUESTIONS

Rodchenko

Retro Bold

CHANGE

East Bloc

SHOUT

Franklin Gothic

OUTSIDE

Follies

BREAK
RULES

Retro Bold

East Bloc Closed Alt

THE
GRID

D.I.Y.

Rodchenko

87

CONSTRUCTIVISM

Constructivism originated in Russia in the 1920s, and is recognized for its visual style of dynamic, angular shapes and flat colours. Typography is combined with perspective and placed alongside photography to give the impression of shouting, or it is placed at angles to make it look like the words are coming right out of the page.

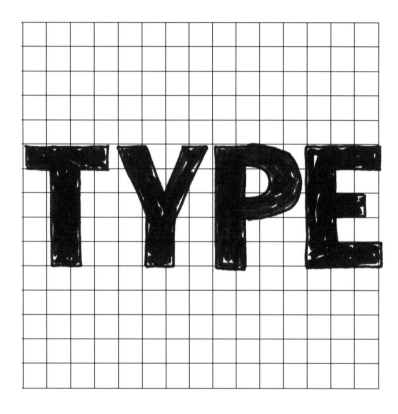

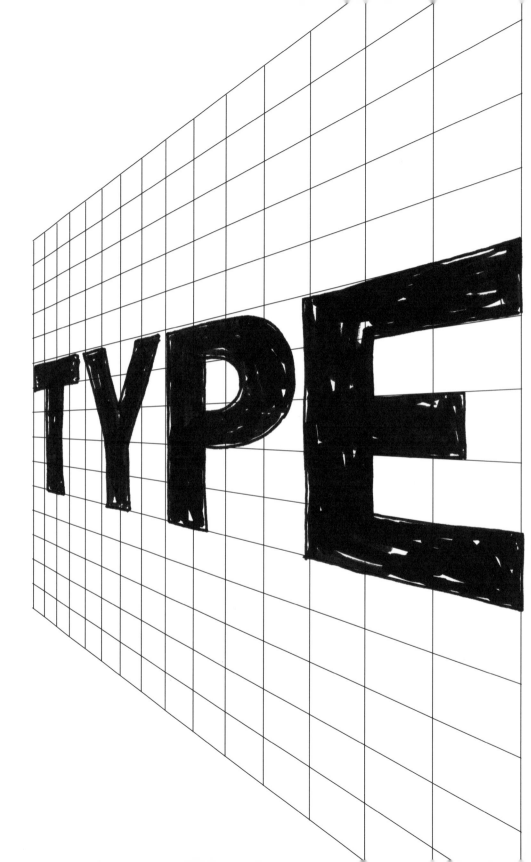

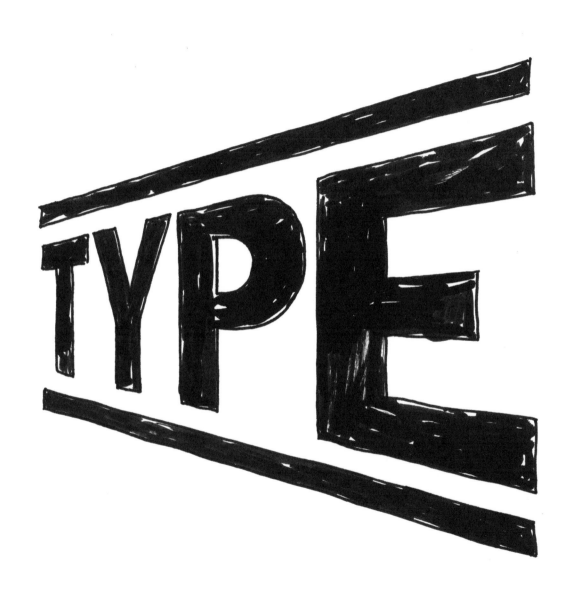

ADDING PERSPECTIVE

1. Think of a word.

2. Draw it on the square grid below (a) in a bold and rebellious typeface style.

3. Reproduce this on the angled grid to the right (b), following the angled lines to add perspective to your word.

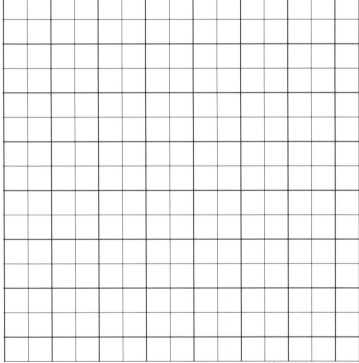

a

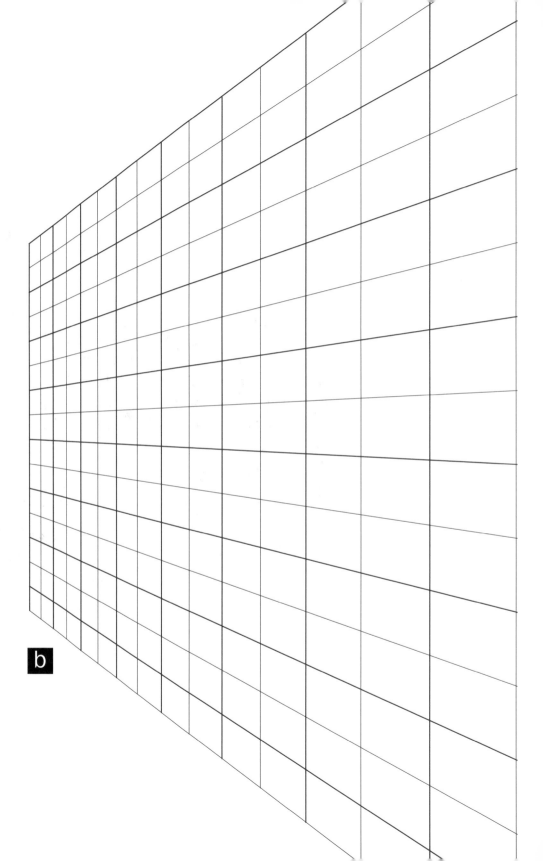

b

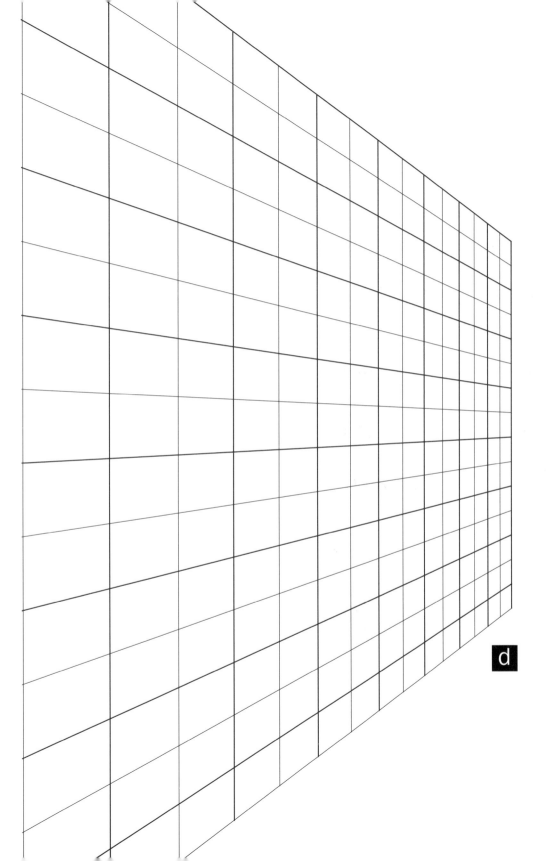

d

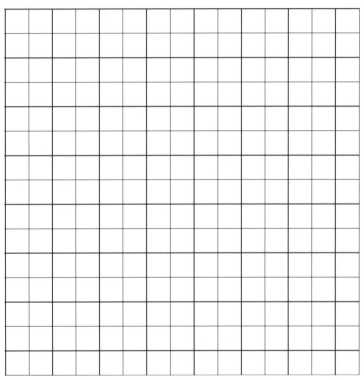

c Repeat the exercise here. Draw your word on the square grid above (c) and then reproduce it on the angled grid on the left (d). Try a different style of typeface.

DADA

Dada was an art movement of the early 20th century. Its followers rejected logic and embraced chaos and irrationality in art, calling for a 'typographical revolution'. Instead of being bolted into rigid typesetting grids, letters were treated as if they were images and were free to be placed anywhere on the page and at any angle.

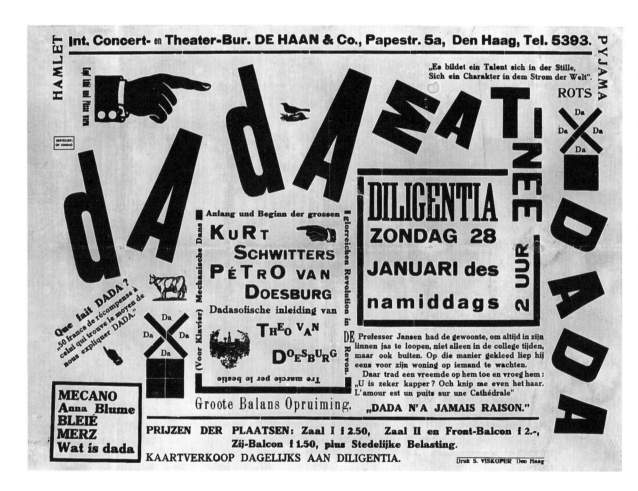

'Dada Matinée', poster by Theo van Doesburg, 1923. To see more Dada typography, do an online search for the typography of Theo van Doesburg and Kurt Schwitters.

Continue your Dada poem across these pages

I COME FROM OUTER SPACE

Use these typefaces to create a stylized glimpse of the future, or to reflect a nostalgic Space Age from times gone by.

Some typefaces, such as Eurostile, have come to epitomize the sci-fi film genre. From visions of utopian hope to those of dystopian struggle, typefaces can reflect many stories.

Franosch

I COME FROM

FUTURE PAST

U T O P I A

EXPLORATION

ROBOT

retro

DYSTOPIAN

QUEST

▥ CMC 7   *F* Sonic   U Futura Light   ⊆ Space Age   ╬ custom lettering   P Amelia   𝘋 Dex Gothic   Q Eurostile Extended

SCI-FI FONTS

Sci-fi typefaces come in a wide assortment of shapes and styles, from the minimalist angular shapes that look like alien symbols, to the retro curves of 1970s' styles. What they all have in common is that they look geometrically constructed, as if either created by a machine or viewed on a computer screen.

The font **CMC 7** looks like it is being beamed from space as the letter begins to materialize.

The sloping, geometric letters of **Sonic** are familiar from the title credits of a famous sci-fi series or movie – can you recognize which one?

The geometric typeface **Futura Light** has appeared in many sci-fi films over the years and has become one of the 'corporate fonts' of sci-fi. The lightweight letters, which allow the background to show through, suggest hope and optimism.

The extended and curved letters of **Space Age** look like a company logo from the future and suggest corporate space exploration.

This custom letter created from a geometric grid looks robotic (see opposite page).

Amelia is reminiscent of computer punch-card type, but its curved shapes suggest the 1960s/1970s and create a 'future nostalgia' feel.

The shapes of **Dex Gothic** look unfriendly and machine-made. They give the impression of a gate or fence barring your way. They suggest a dark future where freedom and liberty may be restricted and a revolution could be on the cards.

Eurostile Extended appeared in the iconic 1969 movie *2001: A Space Odyssey* and has now become a regularly used typeface in the sci-fi genre.

ABCDEFGHI
JKLMNOPQR
STUVWXYZ

Create a futuristic alphabet reminiscent of robots and machines by blocking out sections of the shapes below.

Think of a way to make your alphabet unique. For example, you could do this in a blue pen and use a fluorescent highlighter pen for an illuminated effect.

DESIGN YOUR OWN GEOMETRIC FONT

Group letters that have similar shapes together as you can copy these to make up type families with similar characteristics. You will find that there are base shapes that they all have in common, as shown by the examples below.

For example, the letters B-P-R-S could all be built on the same base shape. Other groups with similar base shapes are E-F-H-L-N-T and C-D-G-O-Q.

Equipment:
Ruler
Protractor
Compass
Pencil

Cap height

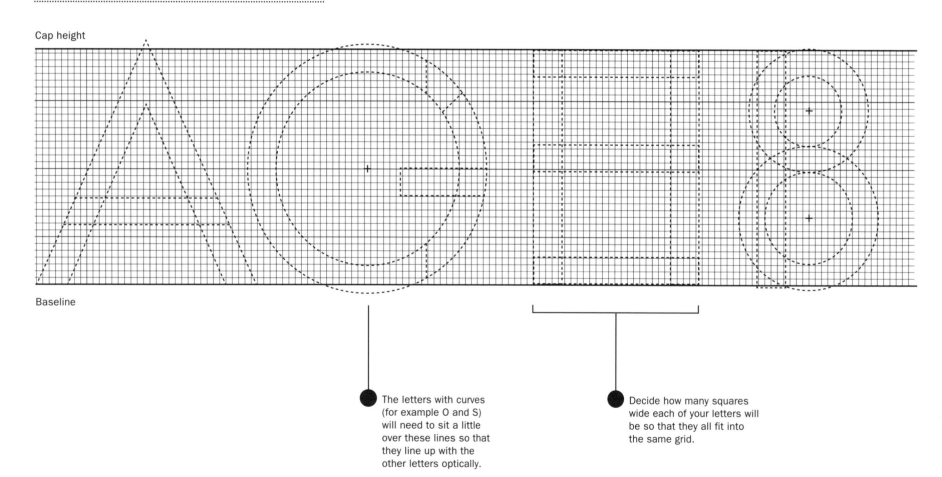

Baseline

The letters with curves (for example O and S) will need to sit a little over these lines so that they line up with the other letters optically.

Decide how many squares wide each of your letters will be so that they all fit into the same grid.

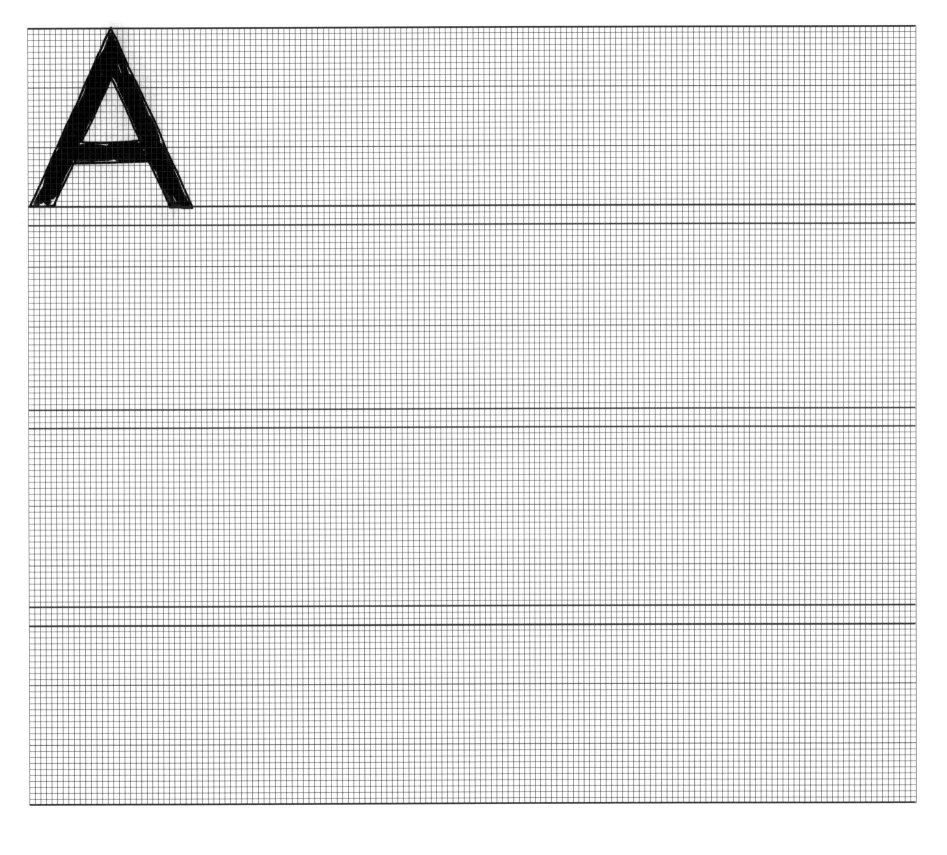

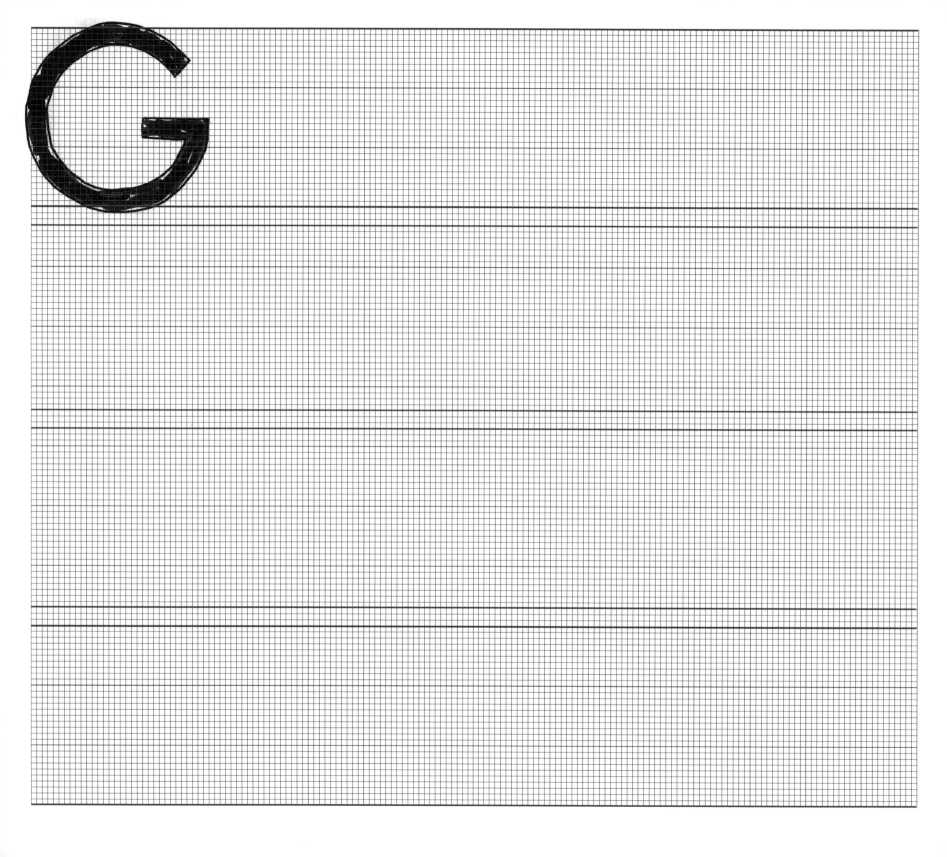

MIXED TYPE

Choose a typeface that adds layers of
meaning to a word, or deconstruct the
letters for an unexpected twist.

Typefaces can turn a word into a story or
they can completely transform its meaning.
They can add humour, create tension or
subvert a message. Create drama by
combining opposites, or make alphabets
with new associations by splicing
letterforms together.

Baskerville + VAG Rounded

CHEAP
Friendly
Shocking
DELICATE
Safe

Top to bottom:
Didot
Klute
Flemish Script
Franklin Gothic Condensed
Bludgeon

ALTERED MEANINGS

Graphic designers sometimes choose typefaces to reflect the meaning of a word, enabling the reader to understand it quickly and easily:

Flemish Script

However, a designer can also select a typeface that conveys something different, extra or surprising, and which creates layered meanings:

Shocking

See the previous page for more examples.

ALTER THE MEANING OF A WORD

1. Choose an adjective or descriptive word.

2. Think of typefaces that have different associations so they alter the meaning of your word in some way.

3. Draw the word in your chosen typeface on the opposite page.

LIST YOUR WORD IDEAS BELOW. WHICH IS YOUR FAVOURITE?

JOT DOWN IDEAS BELOW FOR FONTS THAT WILL CHANGE THE MEANING OF YOUR CHOSEN WORD:

PICK 'N' MIX

Choose two typefaces with different shapes and find a way to splice them together to make a new, hybrid alphabet. This works best if you select very different shapes, for example combining a delicate, ornate script with a chunky stencil typeface.

Edwardian Script   Housebroken

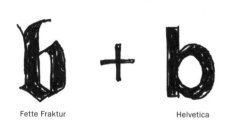

Fette Fraktur   Helvetica

VAG Rounded Bold   Baskerville

Which two typefaces would you combine?   How would you dissect them?   How would you combine the elements?

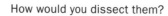

CREATE YOUR
HYBRID ALPHABET

Do you think your new alphabet reflects the personality of the original typefaces, or does it have a new personality of its own?

When could you use this new alphabet?

MASH-UP

A mash-up alphabet takes the pick 'n' mix idea on to the next stage. Think of two fonts with extremely different characteristics and personalities and challenge yourself to create a completely new one that heroes the best (or worst) qualities of both.

For example, artist Mr Cromso was challenged to combine a Blackletter font (Fette Fraktur) with Comic Sans and this is what he created:

Which two typefaces will you challenge yourself to mash together?

Which qualities of each typeface do you plan to hero?

What is the name of your mash-up alphabet?

DRAW THE NAME OF YOUR MASH-UP ALPHABET USING THE LETTERFORMS YOU HAVE DESIGNED:

ANSWERS & RESOURCES

ANSWERS

Trebuchet

Helvetica

Edwardian Script

Umbra

Rosewood

Baskerville Italic

Collaborative studies with the Crossmodal Research Laboratory show that sweet flavours are associated with rounded typefaces, while sour flavours are linked to angular letterforms. In addition, Type Tasting surveys show that crunchy and fizzy taste experiences are associated with angular, bold typefaces.

REFERENCES:

Sarah Hyndman, *Why Fonts Matter*, Virgin Books 2016

Carlos Velasco, Andy Woods, Sarah Hyndman and Charles Spence, 'The taste of typeface design', Crossmodal Research Laboratory 2015

Carlos Velasco, Alejandro Salgado-Montejo, Fernando Marmolejo-Ramos and Charles Spence, 'Predictive packaging design: Tasting shapes, typefaces, names, and sounds', Crossmodal Research Laboratory 2014

Knowledgeable & skilful

Informative & easy

Friendly

Extrovert

Baskerville

Intellectual, academic, wise, knowledgeable

Franklin Gothic

Everyman, doer, dependable, practical

Monotype Corsiva

Artist, idealist, performer, friendly

Bauhaus

Performer, artist, jester, friendly

Caslon

Academic, intellectual, informed, knowledgeable

VAG Rounded

Everyman, idealist, doer, friendly

Bodoni Poster

Performer, leader, idealist, classic

Futura

Idealist, thinker, modern, practical

Braggadocio

Performer, artist, jester, confident

Garamond

Intellectual, thinker, traditional, classic

Cocon

Performer, artist, jester, friendly

Helvetica

Everyman, doer, idealist, neutral

Cinema Italic

Commander, doer, thinker, practical

Georgia

Intellectual, thinker, dependable, classic

Comic Sans

Comedian, everyman, storyteller, friendly

Results taken from the online Type Tasting Font Census. Each typeface has received 250–350 responses. See Sarah Hyndman, *Why Fonts Matter*, Virgin Books 2016

Humanist

Humanist serif typefaces first appeared in the 1470s.

The main characteristics are:

· Calligraphic feel

· Very slanted axis

· Angled crossbar on the 'e'

· Bracketed serifs (curved connection between the stem and the serif)

Old Style

Old Style serif typefaces first appeared in the 1490s.

The main characteristics are:

· Less slanted axis

· Horizontal crossbar on the 'e'

· Bracketed serifs

Transitional

Transitional serif typefaces first appeared in the 1690s.

The main characteristics are:

· Vertical axis

· Horizontal crossbar on the 'e'

· More contrast between thick and thin

· Bracketed serifs

Modern

Modern serif typefaces first appeared in the 1780s.

The main characteristics are:

· Vertical axis

· Horizontal crossbar on the 'e'

· Extreme contrast between thick and thin

· Hairline serifs

· Unbracketed serifs (angled connection between the stem and the serif)

1. WHICH SOUP DO YOU THINK WOULD BE EASIEST TO COOK?

Recipes and instructions are rated as easier to follow when typeset in a sans serif typeface, rather than a serif typeface (of equivalent size and x-height).

2. WHICH SOUP DO YOU THINK WILL BE TASTIEST?

In surveys, the soup described in a script or serif typeface is rated as tastier than the one described in a sans serif typeface of equivalent size.

3. WHICH SOUP ARE YOU MOST LIKELY TO BUY?

This depends on whether you want the soup that is easier to prepare, in which case you are likely to choose the sans serif version, or the soup that is tastier, in which case you are likely to choose the serif version.

Results taken from the Type Tasting online surveys.
Take part at www.bit.ly/TypeTastingLab

A VISUAL TYPE GLOSSARY

TYPOGRAPHY
The art of arranging type.

TYPEFACE
The design of the type family.

TYPE FAMILY
All the fonts within a typeface design.

| Condensed | Light | Roman or Regular | Italic or Oblique | Bold | Extended |

FONT
A font is a computer file or a set of glyphs
in a specific size or weight.

GLYPH
A single character (letter, number,
punctuation mark or symbol).

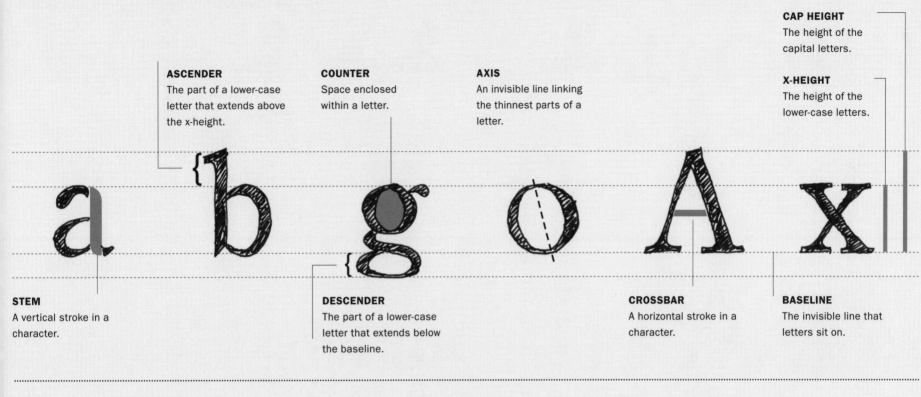

ASCENDER
The part of a lower-case letter that extends above the x-height.

COUNTER
Space enclosed within a letter.

AXIS
An invisible line linking the thinnest parts of a letter.

CAP HEIGHT
The height of the capital letters.

X-HEIGHT
The height of the lower-case letters.

STEM
A vertical stroke in a character.

DESCENDER
The part of a lower-case letter that extends below the baseline.

CROSSBAR
A horizontal stroke in a character.

BASELINE
The invisible line that letters sit on.

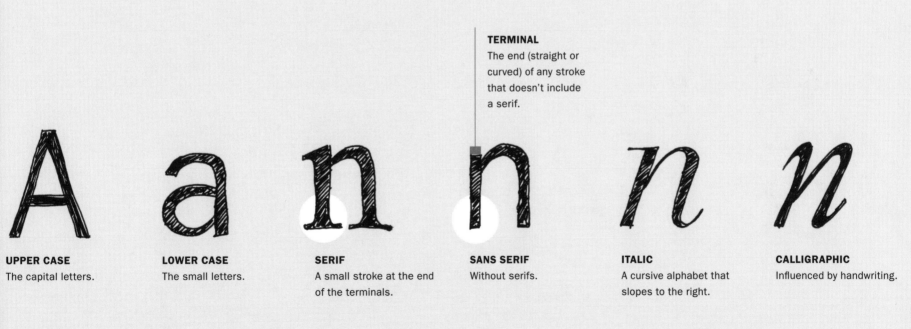

TERMINAL
The end (straight or curved) of any stroke that doesn't include a serif.

UPPER CASE
The capital letters.

LOWER CASE
The small letters.

SERIF
A small stroke at the end of the terminals.

SANS SERIF
Without serifs.

ITALIC
A cursive alphabet that slopes to the right.

CALLIGRAPHIC
Influenced by handwriting.

DOUBLE-STOREY
The a and g have two counters.

SINGLE-STOREY
The a and g have one counter.

BRACKETED SERIF
A curved connection between the stem and the serif.

UNBRACKETED SERIF
The serif connects to the stem at a corner.

HAIRLINE SERIF
Extremely thin serif.

CONTRAST
The contrast between the thick and thin elements of type.

NO CONTRAST

LIGATURE
Two or more letters combined to create a single glyph.

KERNING
The spacing between pairs of letters.

TYPE
Pre-formed letters that can be reproduced identically.

LETTERING
One-off arrangements of letters created by hand.

Legible

Good readability   Po or r ead a bility

LEGIBILITY
How clear the letters
are to read.

READABILITY
The quality of the reading
experience.

HIERARCHY
A system of arranging type
in order of importance.

Headline in display type:

HEADLINE
Sub title

Body copy in a text typeface:

Lorem ipsum dolor sit amet, pellentesque pulvinar sapien ac, magna porta fermentum praesent volutpat. Pellentesque maecenas, dolor non lorem pellentesque. At orci sodales odio non gravida dui, proin mollit curabitur imperdiet, quis etiam sapien augue vel, fusce ante at in in eros, mattis penatibus. Mi etiam mauris fringilla nullam eu magna, ea habitant. Donec fringilla, nunc non nec vitae adipiscing, nam turpis, lacus varius eget mi quis commodo.

RANGED LEFT

Lorem ipsum dolor sit amet, pellentesque pulvinar sapien ac, magna porta fermentum praesent volutpat. Pellentesque maecenas, dolor non lorem pellentesque. At orci sodales odio non gravida dui, proin mollit curabitur imperdiet, quis etiam sapien augue vel, fusce ante at in in eros, mattis penatibus. Mi etiam mauris fringilla nullam eu magna, ea habitant. Donec fringilla, nunc non nec vitae adipiscing, nam turpis, lacus varius eget mi quis commodo.

RANGED RIGHT

Lorem ipsum dolor sit amet, pellentesque pulvinar sapien ac, magna porta fermentum praesent volutpat. Pellentesque maecenas, dolor non lorem pellentesque. At orci sodales odio non gravida dui, proin mollit curabitur imperdiet, quis etiam sapien augue vel, fusce ante at in in eros, mattis penatibus. Mi etiam mauris fringilla nullam eu magna, ea habitant. Donec fringilla, nunc non nec vitae adipiscing, nam turpis, lacus varius eget mi quis commodo.

CENTRED

Lorem ipsum dolor sit amet, pellentesque pulvinar sapien ac, magna porta fermentum praesent volutpat. Pellentesque maecenas, dolor non lorem pellentesque. At orci sodales odio non gravida dui, proin mollit curabitur imperdiet, quis etiam sapien augue vel, fusce ante at in in eros, mattis penatibus. Mi etiam mauris fringilla nullam eu magna, ea habitant. Donec fringilla, nunc non nec vitae adipiscing, nam turpis, lacus varius eget mi quis commodo.

JUSTIFIED

Lorem ipsum dolor sit amet, pellentesque pulvinar sapien ac, magna porta fermentum praesent volutpat. Pellentesque maecenas, dolor non lorem pellentesque. At orci sodales odio non gravida dui, proin mollit curabitur imperdiet, quis etiam sapien augue vel, fusce ante at in in eros, mattis penatibus. Mi etiam mauris fringilla nullam eu magna, ea habitant. Donec fringilla, nunc non nec vitae adipiscing, nam turpis, lacus varius eget mi quis commodo.

Notes

SOME TYPES OF SERIFS

HUMANIST
The first printed Roman typefaces, inspired by the handwriting of Italian Renaissance scholars.

OLD STYLE
More refined letterforms, many of which are still popular today.

TRANSITIONAL
These have a more robust vertical axis, sharper serifs and show the transition from Old Style to Modern.

MODERN
Improvements in technology and paper quality made it possible to print the extremely fine details in these typefaces.

FAT FACE
Extremely bold variation of Modern serifs created for display purposes.

SLAB SERIF
Typefaces with heavy serifs that were often printed at scale and became popular for headlines, billboards and posters.

TUSCAN
A type of slab serif that has rounded or pointed serifs.

ENGRAVED
Inspired by engraved lettering.

GLYPHIC (FLARED)
Often seen carved in stone, the flared shapes of these letters are created naturally by the flow of the signwriter's brush.

SOME TYPES OF SANS SERIFS

Re Re Re Re

GROTESQUE
These are the earliest sans serifs, which look a little like serif typefaces but with the serifs removed.

HUMANIST
These have a hand-drawn feel to their shapes. If you try to draw a sans serif letter in freehand it will most likely reflect the flowing contours of Humanist curves.

GEOMETRIC
These are based on geometric forms. They are sometimes considered to be less readable because the letter shapes look so similar.

NEO-GROTESQUE
These were the first sans serif typefaces to become commercially popular and are associated with Minimalism and the Swiss Modernist movement.

SOME TYPES OF SCRIPT

BLACKLETTER
The first printed styles, which emulated the handwriting of monks and scribes.

FORMAL SCRIPT
A style of script based on the handwriting of master calligraphers.

CASUAL SCRIPT
A script with informal letterforms that appear to have been written quickly.

FURTHER READING

Stephen Coles and Erik Spiekermann, *The Geometry of Type: The Anatomy of 100 Essential Typefaces*, Thames & Hudson 2013

Peter Dawson and Stephen Coles, *The Field Guide to Typography: Typefaces in the Urban Landscape*, Thames & Hudson 2013

FL@33, Tomi Vollauschek and Agathe Jacquillat, *The 3D Type Book*, Laurence King Publishing 2011

Fuse 1–20, Taschen 2012

Simon Garfield, *Just My Type: A Book about Fonts*, Profile Books 2011

Sarah Hyndman, *Why Fonts Matter*, Virgin Books 2016

Alan Kitching and John L. Walters, *Alan Kitching's A–Z of Letterpress: Founts from The Typography Workshop*, Laurence King Publishing 2015

Faythe Levine and Sam Macon, *Sign Painters*, Princeton Architectural Press 2012

Simon Loxley, *Type: The Secret History of Letters*, I.B. Tauris 2006

Ellen Lupton, *Thinking with Type: A Critical Guide for Designers, Writers, Editors and Students*, Princeton Architectural Press 2004

Lars Müller, *Helvetica: Homage to a Typeface*, 2nd rev. edn, Lars Müller Publishers 2005

Josef Müller-Brockmann, *Grid Systems in Graphic Design*, Verlag Niggli 1999

Erik Spiekermann and E.M. Ginger, *Stop Stealing Sheep and Find Out How Type Works*, Adobe 1993

Nikki Villagomez, *Culture + Typography: How Culture Affects Typography*, How Design Books 2015

John L. Walters, *Fifty Typefaces That Changed the World: Design Museum Fifty*, Conran 2013

Steven Heller and Lita Talarico, *Typography Sketchbooks*, Thames & Hudson 2012

BLOGS AND WEBSITES

blog.8faces.com

creativebloq.com

fontshop.com/news

fontsinuse.com

frerejones.com/blog

grafik.net

ilovetypography.com

type-ed.com

typesetinthefuture.com

typetastingnews.com

typewolf.com

typographher.com

INDEX OF TYPEFACES

THANK YOUS

Professor Charles Spence at the Crossmodal
Research Laboratory, University of Oxford.

Carlos Velasco, Daniel Ospina, Nadjib Achaibou,
Chris Lloyd, Andy Woods and the Crossmodalists.

Sign painters Mike Meyer, Sam Roberts of Better
Letters and Ash Bishop of The Brilliant Sign Co.

Bob Richardson and the St Bride Library, London.

Gwendolyn Steele, Caroline Roberts, Nicole A. Phillips,
Anne-Louise Quinton and Geraldine Marshall.

Miho Aishima, Rosalind Freeborn, Syd Hausmann,
Luke Giles, Theo Stewart, Alex Blum and Ed Andrews,
filmmaker.

A special thank you to Monotype for allowing
access to their extensive type library.

Everybody who has participated in Type Tasting
events and research.

Love always to Tina and Terry, and to the generation
of typographers-to-be Clara, Eddie, Dexy, Elle, Owen,
Leon and Stefan.

PICTURE CREDITS

PAGE 58: Pouchée letters courtesy of
St Bride Library and Archives.

PAGE 92: Image and copyright
Centraal Museum, Utrecht.

PAGE 112: Courtesy of Socrome.